I'll Do It Later

Written by Simone T. Ribke · Illustrated by Lee White

Children's Press®
A Division of Scholastic Inc.
New York • Toronto • London • Auckland • Sydney
Mexico City • New Delhi • Hong Kong

To Alan and Michal Reid and all the other little Terps that follow.
I love you.
S.T.R.

For my wonderful wife Lisa and our three silly cats
L.W.

Consultant
Eileen Robinson
Reading Specialist

Library of Congress Cataloging-in-Publication Data
Ribke, Simone T.

I'll do it later / written by Simone T. Ribke ; illustrated by Lee White.
    p. cm. – (A rookie reader)
  Summary: Max avoids doing her chores until her mother tells her they must be done
before she can go skating.
  ISBN 0-516-24861-8 (lib. bdg.)   0-516-25019-1 (pbk.)
  [1. Procrastination–Fiction. 2. Behavior–Fiction.] I. Title: I will do it later. II. White, Lee,
1970- ill. III. Title. IV. Series.

PZ7.R3487Ill 2005
[E]–dc22
                                        2004030130

"I'll do it later," Max always says.

"Max, can you clean your room?
Pick up your airplane, baseball,
basketball, and jewelry box," says Mom.

"I'll do it later," says Max.

"Max, can you rake the leaves in the backyard?"

"I'll do it later," says Max.

8

"Max, don't forget to put some birdseed in Sue's birdcage," says Mom.

"I'll do it later," says Max.

"Max, can you mop up those muddy footprints?"

"I'll do it later," says Max.

"Max, can you put your books
on the bookshelf?"

"I'll do it later," says Max.

"Max, please put your backpack away."

14

"I'll do it later," says Max.

15

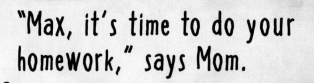

"Max, it's time to do your homework," says Mom.

16

"I'll do it later," says Max.

17

"Max, can you get the mail from the mailbox?"

"I'll do it later," says Max.

"Mom, I'm going out to skate," says Max.

"You are not going anywhere. You can go out after you do all of your chores," says Mom.

Max races to clean her room.

She puts her backpack away.

Max puts her books away, too.

She mops the floor.

Max rakes the leaves.

She does her homework, too.

29

"It's bedtime, Max," says Mom.
"I'll do that now," says Max.

Word List (75 words)
(Words in **bold** are compound words.)

after	books	going	mop	room
airplane	**bookshelf**	her	mops	says
all	box	**homework**	muddy	she
always	can	I'll	not	skate
and	chores	I'm	now	some
anywhere	clean	in	of	Sue's
are	do	it	on	that
away	does	it's	out	the
backpack	don't	jewelry	pick	those
backyard	floor	later	please	time
baseball	**footprints**	leaves	put	to
basketball	forget	mail	puts	too
bedtime	from	**mailbox**	races	up
birdcage	get	Max	rake	you
birdseed	go	Mom	rakes	your

About the Author
Simone T. Ribke is a writer and editor of children's books. Since earning a B.S. in Elementary Education, she has written a wide array of children's and professional education materials. Originally from Maryland, she now lives in New York City.

About the Illustrator
Lee White lives in sunny South Pasadena, California. He spends his days creating whimsical characters and worlds that end up in magazines and books.